Dead Funny

Fritz Spiegl was born in Austria but came to England as a child, went to Magdalen College School, trained both as a typographer and at the Royal Academy of Music, and played first flute with the RLPO for fifteen years. He composes disposable music like TV jingles – and is described as the musician with the widest extra musical accomplishments. As well as being a writer and broadcaster (for seven years regularly with *Start the Week*, since 1970 weekly in the *Liverpool Daily Post* and regularly in *The Listener*) he writes and talks about English language useage, composes humorous verse and gives concerts. His acquired skills range from plumbing to linguistics, from cooking to inventing (one registered patent so far), printing and building. He and his wife recently built a small house from redundant Georgian materials in the gardens of their big old house, which is in the rolling acres of parkland in much-maligned Toxteth. His books include a treatise on Scouse, on newspaper English, and, of course, *A Small Book of Grave Humour* (also published by Pan Books).

Also by Fritz Spiegl
in Pan Books

A Small Book of Grave Humour

Dead Funny

A Second Book of
Grave Humour

edited by
FRITZ SPIEGL

and recreated by
JANE KNIGHTS

Pan Original
Pan Books London and Sydney
by arrangement with the Scouse Press, Liverpool

First published 1982 by Pan Books Ltd,
Cavaye Place, London SW10 9PG
© Fritz Spiegl 1982
ISBN 0 330 26828 7
Printed in Great Britain by
Richard Clay (The Chaucer Press) Ltd, Bungay, Suffolk

WHEN I look upon the tombs of the great, every emotion of envy dies in me; when I read the epitaphs of the beautiful, every inordinate desire goes out; when I meet with the grief of parents, upon a tombstone, my heart melts with compassion; when I see the tomb of the parents themselves, I consider the vanity of grieving for those, whom they must quickly follow. When I see kings lying by those who deposed them; when I consider rival wits placed side by side; or the holy men, that divided the world with their contests and disputes; I reflect, with sorrow and astonishment, on the little competitions, factions, and debates of mankind. When I read the several dates of the tombs, of some that died yesterday, and some six hundred years ago, I consider that great day when we shall all of us be contemporaries, and make our appearance together.

Joseph Addison (1672–1719)
in *The Spectator*

Introduction

Death is no laughing matter but laughter can be therapeutic, especially when it is close to tears. I can think of no better send-off, when I die, than to suffer the kind of mishap which posthumously befell the well-known writer and music critic, Eric Blom (1888–1959). Before his death he had let it be known that the music he wished to have played at his funeral was a Bach chorale, 'I step before Thy throne, Lord God', which the composer himself so poignantly placed at the end of his *Art of Fugue*, whose final, crowning movement he had not had the strength to finish. It is a glorious, chromatic, sad yet confident statement of faith and the perfect choice for any musician's funeral. There would be an organ at the crematorium so a Bach chorale would pose no problem. Came the most solemn moment in the service, and the organ rang out, in the brashest fortissimo of a mighty Wurlitzer:

The resident organist had misheard his instructions and instead of a Bach chorale, played the famous 'Barcarolle' from Offenbach's *Tales of Hoffmann*.

Much of the humour found on gravestones, too, is of the unintentional kind — the unfortunate juxtaposition, for example, of such stock phrases as 'Of such is the Kingdom of Heaven' or 'Well done, good and faithful Servant'.

Fortunately the cutting of letters in stone is a highly skilled, slow and laborious process, so that single-letter mistakes, which can play such havoc with meaning in English, are rare: they will have been spotted before the chisel has cut too far. Typesetting, on the other hand, has lately changed from 'hot', cast type to 'cold' type, and the trade is open to anyone who can cope with the ordinary typewriter keyboard. And it shows. Newspaper misprints abound, and — sad as it is for those closely affected — death announcements are not immune to the slapdash carelessness (in some cases near-dyslexia) now so common wherever print is handled.

> ...ription. On All Hallows' Eve A.D. 1872, this stone was laid by John Bibby, of Hart Hill, who built and endowed this church to the glory of God and in memory of his beloved wide Fanny, who was born on All Hallows'

> WILSON, Arthur. On July 24th in his 88th year, Arthur Wilson, father of Gladys and Richard and grandfather of Jeremy, Tracy, Ann and Sally. PEACE AT LAST.

BERKSWORTH, Arthur.—In loving memory of a dear husband and dad. Died February 14th, 1965. Always in our thoughts.—From his loving wife Mag, Brian and Reg. Accept £38, no dealers.—Write Box A2603, Gazette Office, Epping.

ARTER, In loving

___, George In loving memory of a very dead Dad, who died April 20th, 1956. "Gently the leaves of memory fall

CHURCH NEWS
Former Kinlochbervie Minister Dead

The Rev. John Macaskill, who was Church of Scotland minister at Kinlochbervie, North-West Sutherland, for 50 years, died yesterday at his home there at the age of 88.

A native of Harris, he went to Kinlochbervie as an assistant. He is survived by his wife and one sin.

The terror of sudden, unexpected and often violent death always provided epitaph writers with good *memento mori* material, ostensibly put into the mouth of the deceased: 'What I am now/So thou shalt be/ Prepare ye then/To follow me,' etc., is a recurring example. The very terseness of the inscriptions often matches the suddenness of the melancholy event. People always say 'I'd like to go quickly and suddenly,' but, when the time comes, there are few who do not put up a struggle. This is exemplified by an old Jewish anecdote;

'I wish you should live to a hundred years — plus a fortnight.'

'Why the fortnight extra?'

'Well, I wouldn't wish you should die *suddenly*!'

The inscriptions in this book, some of them lovingly reconstructed by Jane Knights, others set in type, will be found to fall into groups of related material; trades and professions; spouses and siblings; soldiers and sailors; and puns upon names — the last one broadening into inscriptions that reflect the Englishman's inveterate love of playing with words, from feeble, predictable and groanmaking puns to complicated anagrams and rebuses.

It is no coincidence that the most modern epitaph in the book dates from as long ago as the end of the last century, and even that one is dedicated to the memory of a marauding, sheep-worrying dog. For the church authorities no longer sanction any suggestion of levity and indeed publish strict rules governing permissible valedictory texts for fear of offending — or amusing — the living. And one can see how this came about. Some old inscriptions are brutally frank, others scurrilous and doubtless actionable, could the dead but sue. Which incumbent, for example, would now permit the punning tribute to the sexual desirability of Mrs Roger Martin? Or worse, the celebrated musical epitaph by the London composer of Italian extraction, Felice Giardini (1716–1769) on an Earl of Lincoln? It really has to be sung to bring out its full meaning:

Epitaph

Sigr. Giardini

1ˢᵗ Be-neath this Stone the Earl of Lin — coln lies, who

2ᵈ His fate I en-vy and shall and shall think it hard when I

3ᵈ His fate I en-vy and shall and shall think it hard when I

dug who dug his Grave who dug his Grave who

die to be bu — ried in a Count in a Count

die to be bu — ried in a Count in a Count

dug his Grave be — — twixt his La — — dy's

in a Count in a Count in a Count in a Count in a

in a Count in a Country Church Yard when I die to be

Thighs his La dy's Thighs his La — — — dy's Thighs

Count in a Count in a Country Church Yard a Country Churc Yard

bu — ried in a Country Church Yard in a Country ChurchYard

This volume also features a Pets' Corner, including the music Haydn composed for the inscription to his colleague Rauzzini's dog in Bath; as well as a long and touching eulogy on one Fido, whose excellent qualities are somewhat grudgingly admitted in spite of his foreign extraction. Most animal eulogies I have encountered are, of course, to dogs — a tradition that goes back to medieval and even Roman times. The funerary effigies of knights usually include a representation of a lap-dog at the feet of the recumbent figures; and in the Fitzwilliam Museum, Cambridge, there is a gravestone dating from the first century AD showing a distressed dog trying to wake his deceased mistress, Pompeia Margaris. And Byron composed, and had inscribed over his pet's tomb at Newstead Abbey, a florid ode to his Newfoundland dog, Boatswain, who died on 18th November 1808. However, I must confess to some blind prejudice which compelled me to exclude, without malice, Edinburgh's most famous monument to canine obtuseness, for that is how I see it. 'Greyfriars Bobby', it will be recalled by all doggy people, sat for six long years on the cold grave of his master without realizing that the man was no longer in a position to countermand his previous order. Nor is there — and here is the root of my prejudice — any mention on his monument of how Bobby would have turned the adjacent pathways of Greyfriars Churchyard into a disgusting health hazard for other mourners . . . Now a *cat* in a similar predicament would not only have been fastidious about his personal hygiene but, being a more intelligent and sensible creature, might have waited for his master, say, twenty minutes — and then attached himself to the nearest person willing to provide him with food, affection and warmth. It is my fervent hope that when I am dead my relicts will do likewise. But I have yet to find an epitaph to a cat. In desperation I was almost tempted to include Thomas Hardy's 'Last Words to a Dumb Friend' (1904) because, for once, the dumb friend in question was a cat, a species whose devotion, as everyone knows but many refuse to acknowledge, is far more 'human' and loving than the damp-eyed and unquestioning loyalty of the dog, the poem beginning

Pet was never mourned as you,
 Purrer of the spotless hue,
Plumy tail, and wistful gaze
 While you humoured our queer ways . . .

. . . but the whole would not only have been too long but also too painful and harrowing for sensitive cat-lovers to read.

The loss of a beloved pet – usually a dog or a cat but even such apparently emotionless creatures as a parrot or tortoise – who has been a close companion for many years of a probably lonely and elderly person can produce all the distressing symptoms of human bereavement, as doctors well recognize. Dr Kenneth Keddie, in the British *Journal of Psychiatry* (reported in the *British Medical Journal* 30 July 1977) writes of three patients who became 'severely depressed after the deaths of their dogs, and two needed inpatient treatment. All three improved with specific drug treatment.' Relapse was prevented – 'by replacement dogs'. This condition had been recognized at least a century earlier by Alfred Scott Gatty, in his song 'The Poodle', whose mistress found the death of her pet almost unbearable, at any rate for a few weeks:

Then she fretted and she fretted, but all alas in vain;
    So she made a vow she never would keep poodle
    dogs again.
But how weak is human nature: ere three months had
    quickly passed,
    She had bought another poodle dog, exactly like
    the last.

For this second volume of *Grave Humour* I have been able to cast my net wider than for the first. Several early sources, some from abroad, have come to light. I was able to seek out further surviving gravestones, often with the help of readers of the first book, who kindly drew my attention to them. Some of my newly-rediscovered sources go back to the early eighteenth century. The source books include the Greyfriars Records of Edinburgh as well as the meticulous collections (both in print and manuscript) of such early antiquaries as Webb, Toldervey, Hackett and — most scholarly of all — the Reverend Thomas Raven-shaw. I am grateful also to Miss Caroline Hobhouse for setting me on a long trail that led to the delightful eighteenth-century Barbadian Benjamin Massiah. He was by trade a merchant in Bridgetown, but his sideline was the art of circumcision, which he performed 'With Great Applause'. I eventually tracked him down with the further help of Mr Edwin Ifill of the Barbados Public Library. The 'Spiritual Railway' epitaph, dating from 1845, when England was in the grip of railway fever, is reproduced by kind permission of the Dean and Chapter of Ely Cathedral; and my thanks are also due to Mrs C. Proctor, of the Friends of the Cathedral.

As the book has been researched piecemeal and in a desultory fashion over the dozen years or so, I have felt justified in ignoring the foolish counties reorganization of 1974. So far as I am concerned, Rutland, Cumberland, Caernarvonshire and the Yorkshire Ridings are still to be found where they were for over 1000 years; East Bergholt is in Suffolk, not in North-East Humberside or wherever obtuse officialdom has now moved it, and the area known as Deeside remains on the banks of the River Dee, not on 'Merseyside', where it patently and geographically is not.

This collection of epitaphs is dedicated to the compilers and presenters of certain radio and television quiz shows and panel games — notorious scavengers of living men's work, which is then re-anthologized anew under their own names as the inevitable 'Book of the Programme'. This little volume, like some of my previous anthologies, should help to keep them in business for some years to come. However, I am bound to confess that in order to protect the copyright of this compilation I have here and there planted small deliberate mistakes to discourage poachers — a kind of *memento moris*.

Toxteth, Liverpool, March 1982   Fritz Spiegl

RIP

A girl in our village makes love in the
    churchyard,
She doesn't care who, but it must be the
    churchyard.
They say she prefers the old part to the
    new.
Green granite chippings, maybe,
Rankle. Worn slabs welcome.
And after, in her bedroom,
She sees the mirror's view
Of her shoulder embossed
𝔍𝔫 𝔏𝔬𝔳𝔦𝔫𝔤 𝔐𝔢𝔪𝔬𝔯𝔶.

Ann, why do you do it, you've eight 'O'
    Levels?
Why not, Ann? If bones remember, you'll
    give them joy.
It's as good a place as any,
Close by nave, rood screen, chapel at ease,
Peal of the bells,
Bob Singles and Grandsire Doubles,
And when you half close your eyes,
The horned gargoyles choose.

But it has to happen.
Oh, Ann, tonight you were levelled.
𝔚𝔦𝔩𝔩𝔦𝔞𝔪 𝔍𝔬𝔫𝔢𝔰, 𝔩𝔞𝔱𝔢 𝔬𝔣 𝔱𝔥𝔦𝔰 𝔭𝔞𝔯𝔦𝔰𝔥,
Was cold beneath you, and his great-great-
    grandson
Warm above; and you rose,
Though your shoulder didn't know it,
𝔍𝔫 𝔊𝔩𝔬𝔯𝔦𝔬𝔲𝔰 𝔈𝔵𝔭𝔢𝔠𝔱𝔞𝔱𝔦𝔬𝔫 𝔬𝔣 𝔱𝔥𝔢 𝔏𝔦𝔣𝔢
    𝔱𝔬 𝔆𝔬𝔪𝔢.

Whoever is seen loitering
in the Churchyard or behaving
indecently in the Church during
DIVINE SERVICE
will be prosecuted
according to Law

Egloshayle Church, Wadebridge, Cornwall

St George's in the East, London

NO DOGS OR WOMEN
WITHOUT HATS
ALLOWED IN THIS
CHURCHYARD

Camelford, Cornwall

George Warmington
Gent.

of Camelford 5ᵗʰ Jany 1727

Tis my requeſt
My bones may reſt
Within this cheſt
Without moleſt

In memory of

The Rev. *Dr.* THOMAS SHERRIDAN.

Beneath this Marble Stone
There lies
Poor Tom,
More merry much than wife;
Who only liv'd
For two great Ends,
To ſpend his Caſh,
and loſe his Friends.
His darling Wife,
Of him bereft,
Is only griev'd—
There's Nothing left.

From an eighteenth-century collection,
location unknown.

Upon an Orange Merchant, who died in his firſt Wife's Arms upon his Wedding Night.

Alas! Alas! here free from
   Cares and Strife,
Lies one embrac'd to Death
   by his firſt Wife;
Had'ſt thou been ſour as
   Perſian Lemons are,
Thou had'ſt not met a Fate
   ſo ſharp, ſo rare:
But as thou waſt an Orange,
   thou art dead,
For Women love ſuch Sweetneſs,
   e'en in Bed;
And ſhe, who by thee chanc'd
   that Night to lie,
Taſted thee, found thee ſweet,
   and ſuck'd thee dry.

This epitaph is probaby a fanciful invention and may never have appeared on a gravestone. But posthumous candour was often permitted by parsons of the past.

Westham, Essex

Mr. Thomas Warner

who died
Sept. 4ᵗʰ 1787 aged 53

Our life hangs on a single thread
Which soon is cut & we are dead
Then boaſt not reader of thy might
⌐ Alive at noon & dead at night

This epitaph has been variously attributed to churchyards in Warwickshire and Worcestershire, one in Walford Magna and the other in Great Walford. But it survives in neither, so there may well have been some confusion on the part of an eighteenth-century collector of inscriptions.

Here old
JOHN RANDALL lies
Who counting from his tale
Lived three score years and ten
Such virtue was in Ale.
Ale was his meat,
Ale was his drink
Ale did his heart revive:
And if he could have drunk his Ale
He still had been alive:
But he died January five
1699

Eastbourne, Sussex *Prodigy* is here used in the original sense of the word, meaning monstrous or enormous, rather than the modern one denoting precocious gifts found in the young. *Moonshine* is, of course, illicitly distilled or smuggled liquor: 'the white brandy smuggled on the coasts of Kent and Sussex' (Grose's Dictionary of the Vulgar Tongue, 1796). *Sol*: the sun.

THOMAS LOCK
Fisherman of East-Bourne

YE men of *East-Bourne*, and the neighbouring shore,
Bewail your loss! *Tom Lock*—he is no more!
Where will ye find a man of equal parts,
Vers'd in the boatman's and the kitchen arts?
Equally skilful, if at land or sea,
And to behold a perfect prodigy.
His neck distended to uncommon size,
His croaking voice, and then his swollen eyes
Were such true emblems of the life he led,
You'll not much wonder that he now lies dead.
'Twas *moonshine* brought him to this fatal end,
Not one dark night did e'er poor *Tom* befriend!
In vain for him did Sol his light display,
'Twas *moonshine* either night or day.

Beneath this Steane
Lies our dear Child,
Who's gone from We,
For evermore,
Unto Eternity;
Where Us do hope,
That Us ſhall go to He;
But Him can ne'er
Go back again to We.

Wiltshire In small communities the local stone-
mason would often exercise such simple poetic
gifts as he possessed, if necessary at the expense
of grammar.

Reader paſs on
nor idly waſt your time
In bad biography
or bitter rhyme
What I am
this cumbrous clay inſures
And what I was
is no affair of yours

Peterborough, Huntingdonshire

Here lyes, the Lord have
    Mercy on her!
One of her Majesty's Maids
    of Honour;
She was both slender, tall,
    and pretty,
She died a Maid, the more's
    the Pity.

———◆———

An Epitaph answered by a Gentleman on the Widower's Marrying again in a Fortnight.

For me deceas'd weep not, my Dear,
I am not dead, but sleeping here:
Your Time will come, prepare to die;
Wait but a while, you'll follow I.

Answer.
I am not griev'd, my dearest Life;
Sleep on—I've got another Wife:
And therefore cannot come to thee,
For I must go to Bed with she.

From an eighteenth-century collection, where its provenance is given as 'a churchyard in Dorsetshire'.

Stanwick, Northamptonshire The final
quatrain is found in several epitaphs of the period.

IN MEMORY OF

Cheyney Clark

Who died December the 9th 1766

Aged 69 years

This World's a City full of crooked streets
Death is the Market place where all men meet
If Life was Merchandize that men could buy
The Rich would always live and the poor muſt die

Chapel-en-le-Frith, Derbyshire

IN MEMORY

OF

JOHN SHIRT

OF THE WASH

WHO DIED JUNE 5TH 1871
IN HIS 80TH YEAR

ALSO ANN HIS WIFE
WHO DIED MAY 11TH 1830

MR. JOHN MOLE,
d. 24th March 1756

BENEATH this cold stone
Lies a son of the Earth;
His story is short,
Though we date from his
    birth;
His mind was as gross
As his body was big;
He drank like a fish,
And he ate like a pig.
No cares of religion,
Of wedlock, or state,
Did e'er, for a moment,
Encumber John's pate:
He sat, or he walk'd,
But his walk was but
    creeping,
And he rose from his bed
—When quite tir'd of
    sleeping.

Without foe, without
    friend,
Unnotic'd he died;
Not a single soul laugh'd
Not a single soul cried.
Like his *four-footed*
    namesake,
He dearly lov'd earth,
So the sexton has cover'd
His body with turf.

Worcester Playing with the deceased's name was
the most common graveyard sport of all.

Ellen Refon.

The Charnel mounted on the W
Sits to be feen in Funer
A Matron plain, Domeftic
In care and pains continu
Not flow, not gay, nor prodig
Yet neighbourly and hofpit
Her children vii yet liuing
Her 67th yeare hence did c
To reft her bodye natur
In hope to rife fpiritu

} ALL

Hadleigh, Suffolk Here the stone-mason was not being facetious, but was probably saving his time — and his customer's money.

John Rosewell
1687

This grave's a bed of roses
here doth ly
John Rosewell, Gent.
his wife, nine children by

Aetatis suae 79
Obijt 1 Decemb. anno 1687

Jonathan Remnant, *Undertaker*.

Is Remnant gone! Each weeping Eye
  Confirms the mournful Tale;
He, who oft heard the deep-fetch'd Sigh,
  Now bids our Grief prevail.

But ceaſe, ye mourning Friends, to weep:
  Be on his Stone engrav'd,
"God has ordain'd, of thoſe who ſleep,
"A *Remnant* ſhall be fav'd."

Location unknown

Thoˢ Miles
died 7ᵗʰ July 1782

This tombstone is a Milestone—Hah! how so?
Because beneath lies Miles—who's Miles below.
A little man he was, a dwarf in size,
But now stretch'd out, at least Miles long he lies;
His grave, tho' small, contains a space so wide,
'T has Miles in length, and Miles in breadth and
  Miles in room beside.

City of London, from a now demolished church.

Here lieth
JOAN ONELY
the onely
moſt faithful
Wife of
JOHN ONELY
of Warwickſhire,
Eſq.
to whoſe
Soul
the onely
Trinity be merciful.

St John's, Hackney, London

Tho.s More
died 17   May 1760

Stay here awhile,
And his fad fate deplore,
Here lies the body of
One *Thomas More*;
His Name was *More*,
But now it may be faid
He is no more,
Becaufe that now he's dead,
And in this place doth
Lye fepulchared.

Barking, Essex

HERE LYES one *More*
& no more than he
One more & no more —
how can that be
One *More* & no more
may well lye here alone
But here lyes one more
& that is more than one

THOS. MORE
18th June 1670

St Benet's City of London The family names More, Moore, etc., were favourite subjects for epitaph punsters.

Formerly in the Churchyard of Old Bethlem, London Lodowicke Muggleton, with John Reeve, in 1651 or thereabouts founded a sect of religious fanatics who were known as Muggletonians. He and Reeve claimed to be the 'two witnesses' of Revelations, Chapter 11, together with all their supernatural powers ('to shut heaven, that it rain not . . .' and 'if any man will hurt them, fire proceedeth out of their mouth,' etc). Their adherents believed it all and doubtless became the original, over-credulous 'mugs'. The last Muggletonians did not die out until well after the middle of the nineteenth century.

LODOWICKE MUGGLETON

*Who died Monday, March 24, 1698, in the 80th
year of his age.*

*Whilst mausoleums and large inscriptions give
   Might, splendor, and past death make potents live,
It is enough to briefly write thy name,
Succeeding times by that will read thy fame.
Thy deeds, thy acts, around the globe resound;
No foreign soil where Muggleton's not found.
   Sic transit Gloria Mundi*

11th August 1777

Here lies
THOMAS HUDDLESTONE

Reader, don't smile!
But reflect, as this tomb-stone you view,
That death, who kill'd him, in a very short while
Will *huddle a stone* upon you.

Location unknown *Huddle:* to throw uncere-
moniously down, in a heap, probably related to
hurtle, at any rate in dialect usage.

MEMENTO MORI

JOAN LEY

here ſhe Lay[s] all mold in grave
I Truſt in God her Soul to ſave
And with her Saviour Chriſt
to dwell
And there i hope to Live as
well
This Compoſ[d] by her Gratefull
Huſband

NICHOLAS LEY.

1759

Ilfracombe, Devon

Woolborough, Devon *Acrostic*: A word-game in verse by which the initial letters of each line, read downwards, make a word or, in epitaphs, more often the name of the deceased. If the final letters also make a word it becomes a double acrostic, with the further possibility of a triple acrostic when middle letters serve the same purpose.

For The reLIgoVs LADY LUCy onLy Wife of y^t
Wife sIr rIch ReyneL KnIght Who Left Earth on y^e
ResVreCtion Day, Ap. 18th 1652.

L oe Here ſate Majeſty With Meekneſs Crownd,
V ailed Vnder Reverence was Courtſhip Found
C ompoſed Were All ſuch Graces in Her Mind,
Y ee knew in Morraliſt er Chriſtian ſhind.
R efuge of Strangers, Prophets jointureſs,
E aſy Chirvrgeon, Poore men's Treaſureſs,
Y outh's Awe and Age's Honor; To God when
(N ot Thus to Man) Imployd in Prayers and Penn
E ate Through This Marble, if Time ſhall ſhe hath
L eft Vpon Living Stones her Epitaph.
            Ætatis ſuæ 74.

K ind reader judge, here's underlaid
A hopeful, young, and virtuous maid,
T hrown from the top of earthly pleaſure
H eadlong, by which ſhe gain'd a treaſure
E nvironed with heaven's power,
R ounded with angels for that hour
I n which ſhe fell: God took her home
N ot by juſt law, but martyrdom.
E ach groan ſhe fetch'd upon her bed
R oared out aloud I'm murdered.
A nd ſhall this blood, which here doth lie
N vain for right and vengeance cry?
D o men not think, tho' gone from hence,
A venge God can't his innocence?
L et bad men think, ſo learn ye good
L ive each that's here doth cry for blood.

1648

Stokenham, Devon

SILO PRINCEPS FECIT.

```
T I C E F S P E C N C E P S F E C I T
I C E F S P E C N I N C E P S F E C I
C E F S P E C N I R I N C E P S F E C
E F S P E C N I R P R I N C E P S F E
F S P E C N I R P O P R I N C E P S F
S P E C N I R P O L O P R I N C E P S
P E C N I R P O L I L O P R I N C E P
E C N I R P O L I S I L O P R I N C E
P E C N I R P O L I L O P R I N C E P
S P E C N I R P O L O P R I N C E P S
F S P E C N I R P O P R I N C E P S F
E F S P E C N I R P R I N C E P S F E
C E F S P E C N I R I N C E P S F E C
I C E F S P E C N I N C E P S F E C I
T I C E F S P E C N C E P S F E C I T
```

H. S. E. S. S. T. T. L.

A multiple acrostic on a monument to Prince Silo in the **Church of San Salvador, Oviedo, N.W. Spain.** It can be read in 270 ways, beginning with the bold capital in the centre. The lowest line is an abbreviation of an inscription common on Latin tombs: *Hic situs est Silo, sit tibi terra levis* – Here lies Silo; may the earth lie lightly on him. The heading, **SILO PRINCEPS FECIT,** indicates that Prince Silo, whoever he was, wrote the inscription himself.

Edward	EDWARD LAMBE	Lambe
Ever	ſecond ſon of	Lived
Envied	Thomas Lambe	Laudably
Evill	of *Trimley*	Lord
Endured	Eſquire.	Lett
Extremities	All his dayes	Like
Even	he lived a Batchelor	Life
Earneſtly	well learned in Deveyne	Learne
Expecting	and Common Lawes	Ledede
External	With his councell he	Livers
Eaſe	helped many, yett took	Lament
	fees ſcarſe of any.	

He dyed the 19th of November 1647.

In Memory OF

Ralph Tyer, Vicar of this Parish

London bred me . . . Weſtminſter fed me
Cambridge fped me . . my fiſter wed me
Study taught me . . . living fought me
Learning brought me . Kendal caught me
Labour preſſed me . . ſickneſs diſtreſſed me
Death oppreſſed me . . the grave poſſeſſed me
God firſt gave me . . . Chriſt did ſave me
Earth did crave me . . and . . heaven would have me.

Kendal, Westmorland 1627

TIM-PERL-EY

Lo Time = Pearle = Ey, a Rebus, which to thee
Speakes what I whilom Was, a *Timperley*.
Wing'd Time is flowne, So is yᵉ World from me,
A glitt'ring Pearle, whoſe gloſſe is Vanitie.
But th' Ey of Hope is of a nobler flight,
To reach beyond thee (Death), enioye his ſight
Who conquer'd thee.   Hence ſpring my hopes yᵗ I
Shall riſe yᵉ fame, & more, a *Timperley*.

Depoſita eſt haec Spes mea in ſinu meo.
                    Iob. 19.

Nicolas Timperley, Sonne of Sir Thomas Timperley of
Hintleſham in yᵉ Countie of Suffolke, Knight, dyed Anno
dni. 1658.

Colkirk, Norfolk *Rebus*: Latin, with things:
really 'words with things', often in hieroglyphic
representation.

Theophilus Cave
died 1584

Here in this grave there lies one
    CAVE;
    We call a cave a grave.
If cave be grave, & grave be cave
    Then reader judge I crave
Whether both CAVE lye in this grave
    Or grave here lye in cave;
If grave in cave here buried lye,
    Then grave where is thy victory?
        Go reader and report
        Here lyes a CAVE
        Who conquers death
        And buries his own grave.

Barrow-on-Soar, Leicestershire

Inscription on a gravestone to a Welsh dog shot while attacking sheep. From the **Animals' Garden of Rest,** now the property of Mr Gwilym M. Williams, at **Llanuwchllynn, North Wales.**

RECTOR

AGED 4 YEARS

SHOT
31st MARCH 1890

ATE WITHOUT STINT
LAMB WITHOUT MINT

Bath This canon in four parts was composed by Haydn on a visit to the composer and castrato singer Venanzio Rauzzini (b. Italy 1746, d. Bath 1810) in the summer of 1794. The epitaph to Turk was already in existence when Haydn arrived, on a stone erected in Rauzzini's garden in Bath, and bore the inscription *Turk was a faithful dog, and not a man*. For performance, the second voice should enter when the first reaches the end of the top line, observing the pause ⌒ only at the end of the canon.

To the memory of
SIGNOR FIDO,
An Italian of good extraction,
Who came into England,
Not to *bite* us, like most of his countrymen,
But to gain an honest livelihood.
He *hunted* not after fame,
Yet acquired it.
Regardless of the praise of his friends,
But most sensible of their love.
Tho' he liv'd among the great,
He neither learnt nor flattered any vice.
He was no bigot,
Tho' he doubted of none of the thirty-nine articles:
And if to follow nature,
And to respect the laws of society,
Be philosophy,

He was a perfect philosopher,
A faithful friend,
An agreeable companion,
A loving husband,
And, tho' an Italian,
Was distinguished by a numerous offspring,
All which he liv'd to see take good *courses*.
In his old age he retir'd
To the house of a clergyman in the country,
Where he finish'd his *earthly race*.
And died an honour and an example to the
whole species.
Reader,
This stone is guiltless of flattery;
For he, to whom it was inscrib'd,
Was not a man,
But a GREYHOUND.

In Stow gardens

Memorial stones to dogs, horses and other domestic pets, who naturally kindle love by their affectionate demeanour, are no novelty, but it is indeed unique to find such a token of appreciation extended to a pig. This stone was erected around the turn of the century over the grave of a sow by Mrs A. V. Taylor, of the **Cock Hotel farmstead, Worsley, near Manchester.** It was still in existence in 1905, when a photograph of the monument appeared in the Strand magazine.

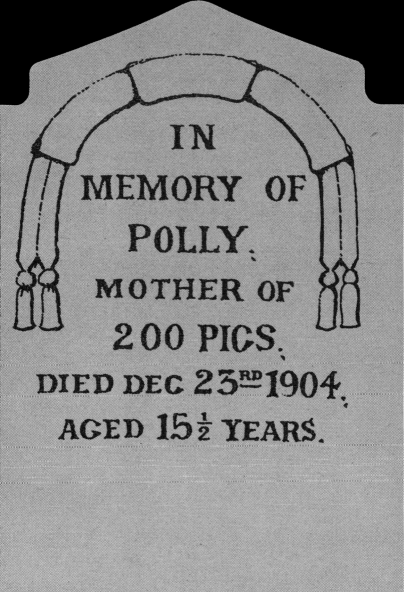

IN
MEMORY OF
POLLY.
MOTHER OF
200 PICS.
DIED DEC 23RD 1904.
AGED 15½ YEARS.

SARAH HALL

To the memory of a young maiden, who was
accidentally drowned December 24 1796

By her Lover

NIGH to the river Ouse, in York's fair city,
Unto this pretty maid death shew'd no pity;
As soon as she'd her pail with water fill'd,
Came sudden death, and life like water spill'd.

St Mary's, York

John Martin
died 8th Novr. 1787

The Lord faw good, I was lopping off wood,
And down fell from the tree:
I met with a check, & I broke my neck,
And fo death lopped off me.

Here lies
Elizabeth Wyse
killed
by thunder
sent from heaven
in 16 hundred
and seventy seven

Here Charles Rathbone he doth lie
And by a misfortune he did die
On the 17th of July.
1751.

St Giles's, Shrewsbury, Shropshire

Milton Regis, Kent Simon Gilker was evidently an early victim of the folly that grips Englishmen every 5th November, when they celebrate the failure of the Catholic Gunpowder Plot of 1605 by setting off small explosive charges in each other's faces. Fawkes's attempt to blow up the Houses of Parliament was foiled without bloodshed, except to himself and his fellow plotters; but he would have been astonished had he known how many Englishmen, both Catholic and Protestant, he was posthumously to maim and kill.

The Rev. W. Drury, Vicar of Milton Regis, suspects that Gilker may have 'borrowed' a rocket from the Navy at Sheerness — and adds that he was one of the churchwardens of the parish at the time of his death.

HERE lyeth the
body of SIMON
GILKER Junior
who was killed by
means of a Rockett
November 5 1696
Aged 48 Years
also the body of
Elizabeth his wife

JOHN WRIGHT
Here lie I
No wonder I'm dead
For a broad wheeled Waggon
Went over my Head.
Grim Death took me
Without a Warning
I was Well at Night
And dead in the Morning.
15 March 1797

Sevenoaks, Kent

An Epitaph, *infcribed on a Pillar lately erected in the Midft of an old Heap of Stones, on the Side of the Highway, in the North of* England. *By the Lord of the Manor.*

Stay, Traveller, ftay, and perufe a fad Story;
For here I am fet, as a *Memento Mori*,
To give the World Notice, that under thefe Stones,
Here lie the Remains of one William Jones,
Who made, if the Tale be as true as 'tis old,
Too much Hafte (alas!) to get rid of a Scold.
One Night, as he under her Difcipline lay,
Atoning for Crimes of the foregoing Day,
An unfortunate Thought came into his Head
To make his Efcape: So he rufh'd out of Bed,
And ran with all Speed to the Brink of yon Delph,
From whence leaping headlong, he brained himfelf.
This was, without Queftion, his own Act and Deed,
And yet in their Cenfures all are not agreed.
The Law, it condmn'd him, you fee here; but ftill
Some People applaud him; Becaufe, fay they, Will
Chofe rather to lie, for avoiding of Strife,
Alone in a Grave, than in Bed with his Wife:
Whilft others entitle him Fool for his Pains,
In dafhing out 's own, instead of her Brains.

Near Preston, Lancashire *Delph* : a village.

AN EPITAPH

ON

OSWALD GARDNER

Locomotive Engineman

WHO UNFORTUNATELY LOST HIS LIFE NEAR THE STOKESFIELD STATION

NEWCASTLE & CARLISLE RAILWAY

FROM THE CONNECTING ROD OF THE ENGINE BREAKING

ON SATURDAY AUGUST 14th 1840

HE WAS TWENTY~SEVEN YEARS OF AGE & WAS HIGHLY
ESTEEMED FOR HIS MANY AMIABLE QUALITIES BY HIS FELLOW~
WORKMEN, & HIS DEATH WILL BE LONG LAMENTED BY ALL WHO
HAD THE PLEASURE OF HIS AQUAINTANCE. THESE LINES WERE
COMPOSED BY AN UNKNOWN FRIEND & LEFT AT THE BLAYDON
STATION; & AS A MEMENTO OF THE WORTHINESS OF THE DEC~
EASED, HAVE BEEN PRINTED, WITH SOME EMENDATIONS,
AT THE EXPENSE OF HIS FELLOW~WORKMEN

My *Engine* now is cold and still
No water does my *boiler* fill
My *coke* affords its flame no more
My days of usefulness are o'er
My *wheels* deny their noted speed
No more my guiding hand they heed
My *whistle*, too, has lost its tone
Its shrill and thrilling sounds are gone
My *valves* are now thrown open wide.
My *flanges* all refuse to guide.
My *clacks* also though once so strong
Refuse their aid in the busy throng
No more I feel each urging breath
My *steam* is now condens'd in death
Life's *railway's* o'er, each *station's* past
In death I'm stopp'd and rest at last
Farewell, dear friends, and cease to weep
In CHRIST I'm SAFE, in HIM I sleep

By the South Door of Ely Cathedral Thomas (not William) Pickering and Richard Hedger (not Edger) were driver and stoker, respectively, on the 11.15 a.m. up train from Norwich on Christmas Eve, 1845. The train ran off the line at the bottom of a 1¾ mile decline between Harling Road and Thetford, on the former Norfolk Railway. 'The accident,' says the Board of Trade accident report dated 1st January 1846, 'was due to the excessive speed of the train in the 1 in 200 falling gradient.' Pickering was reported to have been 'addicted to fast driving'. He was killed immediately, and his fireman died two hours after having a leg amputated. No passengers were seriously hurt in the accident. This illustration is taken, by kind permission of the Dean and Chapter, from the postcard reproduction of the monument on sale at the Cathedral bookstall.

IN MEMORY OF

WILLIAM PICKERING,
who died Dec^R 24. 1845
AGED 30 YEARS

ALSO RICHARD EDGER
who died Dec^R 24. 1845.
AGED 24 YEARS.

THE SPIRITUAL RAILWAY

The Line to heaven by Christ was made
With heavenly truth the Rails are laid,
From Earth to Heaven the Line extends.
To Life Eternal where it ends

Repentance is the Station then
Where Passengers are taken in,
No Fee for them is there to pay
For Jesus is himself the way

God's Word is the first Engineer
It points the way to Heaven so dear,
Through tunnels dark and dreary here
It does the way to Glory steer.

God's Love the Fire, his Truth the Steam,
Which drives the Engine and the Train,
All you who would to Glory ride,
Must come to Christ, in him abide

In First and Second, and Third Class,
Repentance, Faith and Holiness,
You must the way to Glory gain
Or you with Christ will not remain

Come then poor Sinners, now's the time
At any Station on the Line.
If you'll repent and turn from sin
The Train will stop and take you in.

Gravestone No. 367 in the **burial ground of the Jews' Synagogue at Bridgetown, Barbados,** transcribed and translated by E. M. Shilstone.

Underneath this Tomb
lies interred
The Earthly Remains of
Benjn. MASSIAH
Late Merchant of this Island
who was universally
Beloved and Respected by
All that knew him and whose
Death
was much lamented.
He had been Reader of the
JEWS SYNAGOGUE
for many years without Fee or Reward
and performed the Office of
CIRCUMCISER
with Great Applause
and Dexterity.
He departed this life
on the 29 Adar 5542
Corresponding to
the 15th of March
1782
Aged 67 Years and Eight Months

Andrew Meekie, late Parifh Dominie.

Beneath thir ſtanes lye MEEKIE's banes:
   O Sawtan, gin ye tak him,
Appeynt him tutor to your weans,
   An' clever deils he'll mak 'em.

1696

Edinburgh, Scotland *Dominie*—schoolmaster,
tutor. *Sawtan*—Satan. *Weans*—children.

*Thomas Turar twice Maſter of the Company
of Bakers, and twice Churchwarden of this Pariſh*

Like to a Baker's Oven is the grave
Wherein the bodyes of the faithful have
A Setting in, and where they do remain
In hopes to Riſe, and to be Drawn again;
Bleſſed are they who in the *LORD* are dead,
Though Set like Dough, they ſhall be Drawn like Bread.

1st June 1643

Bristol

[Probably fictitious]

Here into duſt
The mouldering cruſt
Of old Bell Bachelor's shoven
She knew well the arts
Of pies cuſtards and tarts
And all the skill of the oven
When she'd liv'd long enough
She made her laſt puff
A puff by her huſband
much praiſed
Now here she doth lie
To make a dirt pie
In hopes
that her cruſt may be raiſed

Henry Hudson
late Hat-Maker

of Fore Street
who Died June 1787
while eating his Breakfast

Ah stamp not rudely on Hal Hudson's bed
Tho' oft he's stampt upon your nation's head
For he was authorized nay forced to do it
Or else he'd been full sorely made to rue it —
Making a meal this good hat-maker died
& merrily 'tis said to his own Maker hied

Lydford, Devon A favourite theme for clock-makers' epitaphs.

Here lies in a horizontal poſition
The outſide caſe of GEORGE RONGLEIGH, Watchmaker,
Whoſe abilities in that line were an honor
to his profeſſion:
Integrity was the Mainſpring
and Prudence the Regulator
of all the actions of his life;
Humane, generous, and liberal,
His Hand never ſtopped
Till he had relieved diſtreſs:
So nicely were all his Actions regulated
That he never went wrong,
Except when ſet a going
By People
Who did not know his key:
Even then he was eaſily ſet right again.
He had the art of diſpoſing his time ſo well
That his hours glided away
In one continual round
of pleaſure and delight,
Till an unlucky minute put a period to
His exiſtence.
He departed this life November 14th, 1802,
aged 57;
Wound up
In hopes of being taken in hand
by his Maker,
And of being thoroughly cleaned and repaired,
And ſet a going
In the world to come.

Location unknown

Hugh Morgan

SLEEPETH HERE IN PEACE:

WHOM MEN DID LATE ADMIRE
FOR WORTHFUL PARTS.
TO QUEEN ELIZABETH
HE WAS CHIEF 'POTHECARY
TILL HER DEATH

And in his science as he did excell
   In her high favour he always did dwell
   To God religious, to all men kind
   Frank to the poor, rich in content of mind
   These were his virtues, in these died he
   When he had liv'd an 100 years and 3

BENEATH the droppings of this spout,
Here lies the body, once so stout,
Of FRANCIS THOMPSON:
A soul this carcase once posses'd
Which for its virtue was caress'd
By all who knew the owner best.
The Rufford records can declare,
His actions, who, for seventy year,
Both drew, and drank, its potent beer.
Fame mentions not, in all that time,
In this great *butler* the least crime
To stain his reputation.
To Envy's self we now appeal,
If aught of fault she can reveal,
To make her declaration.
Then rest, good shade, nor hell, nor vermin fear,
Thy virtues guard thy soul, thy body good strong beer.

Allerton, Nottinghamshire The stone joins the
south wall of the church under one of the spouts.
Rufford Abbey was the seat of Sir George Saville,
Bart., in whose family Thompson had lived as
butler.

JOSEPH WRIGHT
Auctioneer
died 17th November 1818

Beneath this stone, facetious wight,
Lies all that's left of poor Joe Wright.
Few heads with knowledge more informed,
Few hearts with friendship better warmed.
With ready wit and humour broad
He pleased the peasant, squire, and lord;
Until grim death, with visage queer,
Assumed Joe's trade of Auctioneer;
Made him the Lot to practise on,
With "going, going," and anon
He knocked him down to "Poor Joe's gone!"

Corby

Llanbelig, Caernarvonshire

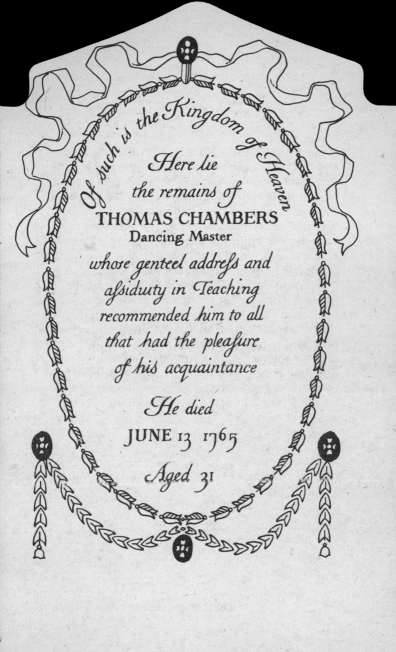

Of such is the Kingdom of Heaven

Here lie
the remains of
THOMAS CHAMBERS
Dancing Master

whose genteel addreſs and
aſsiduty in Teaching
recommended him to all
that had the pleaſure
of his acquaintance

He died
JUNE 13 1765

Aged 31

Anne Catley, 1745–1789, was a famous singer and high-class prostitute, the daughter of a London washerwoman and a coachman. Like many a modern pop singer, the beauty of her face appears to have persuaded her public that her voice, too, was beautiful, and like them, she acquired more fame for her amorous exploits (almost invariably with noble or titled men) than for her singing or acting. She died at the start of the 1789 season at the Covent Garden Theatre, at General Lascelles's house in Brentford, although the epitaph opposite was **engraved on a tree on the Hertfordshire estate of George Stainforth**, whom presumably she also made happy. The last two lines of the extract quoted refer not to her professional prowess but to the fact that she passed on much of her wealth to the poor, leaving for *their* relief £5,000 and some property when she died.

ANNE CATLEY
died 14th Oct. 1789

Catley, the once famed Syren of the stage,
Melodious heroine of a former age,
Her labours o'er, here fix'd her glad retreat;
These her lov'd fields, and this her fav'rite seat.
Hither at early dawn she bent her way,
To mark the progress of the new mown hay;
Partook the toil, joined gaily in the throng,
And often cheer'd the rustics with a song;
Nor with a song alone, her liberal heart
In all their little sorrows bore a part,
And as they simply told their tale of grief,
Her head gave counsel and her hand relief.

Location unknown

1658

ROGER GARDINER & WIFE

Roger lyes here
before his hour
Thus doth Gardiner
lose his flower

16th MAY

Naval cemetery, Antigua, West Indies The visitor to the British graveyard in Gibraltar will find many touching naval epitaphs there too, especially those dedicated to victims of the Battle of Trafalgar.

SACRED
TO THE MEMORY OF

Thomas Wotton A.B.
aged 34
Who was accidentally killed in the
execution of his duty on board
H.M.S. 'Phaeton' *July 28th 1863*

A noble fellow there he stood
With 10 years service 'Very good'
A seaman's pride to firmly make
The bowsprit all its strain partake
A block it split and sprung in two
The angry fragments round him flew
One struck poor Wotton's manly head
And left him bleeding, dying, dead
He's gone from us he's gone from sight
But God is good His judgment right
The just he takes the sinner lives
He loves us all, and all forgives

John Dunch
Capptain Mariner

Though Boreas' blafts and Neptune's waves
   Have toff'd me to & fro:
In fpite of both by Heaven's decree,
   Harbour I here below.
Where I do now at anchor ride
   With many of our fleet:
Yet once again I muft fet faile,
   Our ADMIRAL CHRIST to meet.

Stepney, London Others, with variations, appear in Devon, Suffolk and Kent.

WILLIAM BILLINGS

A soldier, who died at Fairfield near Longnor, in the county of Stafford, at the advanced age of 102, on Friday, January 28, 1791. He was born under a hedge in 1694, not an hundred yards from the cottage where he died, and it is related that he never knew what sickness was, and died without a groan.

Conquests I shar'd
in many a *dreadful scene,*
With matchless Marlbro'
and with brave Eugene,
To peaceful *quarters*
billeted am I,
And here forgetful
of my labours lie.
Let me alone,
awhile asleep, not *slain,*
For, when the *trumpet sounds,*
I'll march again.

St Luke's, Chelsea, London *Virago*: a Latin word denoting 'a mannish woman or female warrior; a bold, impudent or wicked woman; a scold.' (Oxford English Dictionary)

Sacred to posterity.

In a vault, near this place, lies the body of
ANNE, the only daughter of
EDWARD CHAMBERLAYNE, LL. D.
Born in London, January 20, 1667,
Who,
For a considerable time, declined the matrimonial
state,
And scheming many things
Superior to her sex and age,
On the 30th of June, 1690,
And under the command of her brother,
With the arms and in the dress of a man,
She approv'd herself a true VIRAGO,
By fighting undaunted in a fire ship against the
French,
Upwards of six hours,
She might have given us a race of heroes,
Had not premature fate interposed.
She returned safe from that naval engagement,
And was married, in some months after, to
JOHN SPRAGGE, Esq.
With whom she lived half a year extremely happy,
But being delivered of a daughter, she died
A few days after,
October 30, 1692.

This monument, to his most dear and affectionate
wife, was erected by her most disconsolate husband.

St Andrew's Churchyard, Newcastle-on-Tyne

Mary

wife of Robert M'Cutchin
SERGEANT in the GRENADIER GUARDS
died May 11 1781
in the 27th year of her age

In all our marriage vows she did fulfill
And fondly sought her huſband thro' the dead
on Bunker's Hill
At many actions more & at the Brandy-Wine
She lov'd her huſband so
she would not stay behind
Till now by cruel Death's dread dart
She is left behind & forc'd to part
Till the laſt trump when Gabriel sounds amain
She'll riſe, embrace & join again

Beneath this Stone lieth
Interred
The Body of

ROBERT
HIGGINGBOTTOM

Pioneer
of the 1st Regt. of Yorkfhire,
Weft Riding Militia
Commanded by the Honble. Colonel
Sir George Savile, Bart.
and in Capt. Wilmer Goffips Company
who was unfortunately slain in the
prime of life on the evening of the
17th March A.D. 1780
aet. 23 years

He unguardedly went out, with 2 quarts
of ale, from his own quarters,
To a private Houſe in Hackens Hey,
in this Town,
for some sailors, who were drinking &
making merry,
who were immediately attacked by an
armed press gang, by which he
received 2 mortall wounds
The perpetrators of this horrid murder
are as yet undiſcovered
tho by a reſpectable jury was bought in
Wilfull.

This stone was erected to his Memory by the
ſubſcriptions of his Comrades.

St Peter's Churchyard (flattened and built
over in 1921), Church St, Liverpool

Dumfries, Scotland

Here Lies

Andrew Macpherson

Who was a
very peculiar
person
He stood
six foot two
without his shoe
And was slew
At Waterloo

Isle of Man

In memory of

JOHN
REDDISH Esq.
Lieut. Colonel in the army

died 17th MAY 1717
aged 69

When he sought death
with sword & shield
Death was afraid
to meet him in the field
But when his weapons he had
laid aside
Death, like a coward, stroke him
& he died

YET a verie little, and he that will come shall come.
The speritt and the bride say come.
Lett him that heareth say come.
And lett him that is a-thirst say come.
Even so come Lord Jesv.

VRSVLA
{
Tyndall by birth.
Coxee by choice.
Vpcher in age and for comfort.
}
ANNO ÆTATIS 77°·

From a brass plate affixed to a stone in the **Cathedral of Ely,** *between the Monuments of* **Bishop Heton** *and* **Bishop Gunning.**

'N.B. This gentlewoman was the daughter of Doctor Humphrey Tyndall, first Dean of Ely, and was called Sappho from her wit and morals.   She married at twenty, became a widow at forty-two, and after having enjoyed her liberty thirty-five years, married again at seventy-seven, a lad of nineteen, " for comfort, being within two months of her end ".'

In memory of

Sir Lawrence Tanfield
died 1625

Here ſhadows lie
Whilſt earth is ſadd;
Still hopes to die
To him ſhee hadd.

So ſhall I bee
With him I loved;
And he with mee,
And both us bleſſed.

In bliſſe is hee
Whom I loved beſt;
Thrice happy ſhee
With him to reſt.

Love made me poet,
And this I writt;
My heart did do it,
And not my witt.

Written by his Wife

Burford, Oxfordshire

Location unknown *Tissickey*: the word does not appear in the Oxford English, or any other dictionary I consulted, but it is obviously related to the Latin noun *tussis*, a cough.

Below lyes
for sartin
Honest old HARTING
And snug
close beside un
His fat WIFE a wide one
If another you lack
Look down
and see JACK
And farther a yard
Lyes CHARLES
who drank hard
And near t'un lies MOGGY
Who never got groggy
Like Charles & her father
Too abstemious
the rather
And therefore popp'd off
In a tissickey cough
Look round now
& spy
The whole family out

St Nicholas's Church, Worth Matravers, Dorset Ask anyone who made the first practical experiments in inoculation against small pox, and you will be told it was Edward Jenner (1749–1823). The first vaccinator was, in fact, not a medical man at all but a farmer, Benjamin Jesty, who anticipated Jenner by almost a quarter of a century. His story was told by Prof. Bryan Brooke in *World Medicine*, 22nd September 1979, together with a picture of Jesty's birthplace and his tombstone.

(Sacred)

To the Memory

— OF —

Benj^m Jesty.(of Downshay)
who departed this Life,
April 16.th1816.
aged 79 Years

He was born at Yetminster in this
County, and was an upright honest
Man: particularly *noted* for having
been the first Person(known) that
introduced the *Cow Pox*
by *Inoculation,* and who from
his great *strength of mind made the
Experiment from* the (Cow) on
his Wife and two Sons in the Year 1774

Location unknown Eighteenth-century epitaph writers were always ready to suggest a cause of death – however unscientific.

Here lyes EMILY the wife of
EDWARD GREENWOOD DD
died 1 July 1800

O Death O Death thou haſt cut down
The faireſt *greenwood* in the town
Her virtues & good qualities were such
She was worthy to marry a lord or a judge
Yet such was her condeſcenſion & humility
She choſe to marry me a Doctor of Divinity
For which heroic act she stands confeſs'd
Above all women the Phoenix of her sex
And like that bird one young she did beget
That she might not
Leave her friends diſconſolate
My grief for her, alas! is so sore
I can only write two lines more
For this & every other good woman's sake
Never lay a bliſter
on a lying-in woman's back

Great Wilbraham, Cambridgeshire

May this Monument be fustained
To the end of Time
SACRED
To the Memory and Vertues of
Mifs MARY WARD
The Darling of her Friends
The Admiration of Strangers
And real Blessing of her Family.
Her Person
Was tall and gracefull
Her Features
Handfome and Regular
But her Mind
Pious, Modeft, Delicate and Amiable
Beyond the credit of Defcription.
Parents of Children
And Inhabitants of her Native Village
Drop a Tear
To this Sweet Short-lived Flower
Who having juft added a Complete Education
To her natural Excellencies
DIED
Uncommonly Perfect and Lamented
On the 30th Jany.
1756
Aged 15 years 6 months.

To the memory of
JOHN MAGHI,
An incomparable boy,
Who, thro' the unskilfulness of the midwife,
On the 21st day of December, 1532
Was translated from the womb to the tomb.

Location unknown The writer anticipated by some sixty years Shakespeare's line, 'Making their tomb the womb wherein they grew' (Sonnet 86).

Here lies the Body of Joan Carthew,
Born at St. Columb, buried at St Cue;
Children fhe had five;
Three are dead, and two alive;
Thofe that are dead choofing rather
To die with the Mother
Than live with the Father.

St Cue Cornwall

Shrewsbury, Shropshire

In Memory OF

Elizabeth Streven

Who resign'd her soul to Heav^n
Her years were exactly seven
Died 9th May 17 hunder^d & 11

Probably fictitious, but irresistible !

Beneath this sod

lies another

Pravity: from the Latin *Pravitas*, crookedness, distortion, perverseness. It is not the opposite of depravity, but a different form of it, the prefix 'de-' being an intensification, not a negation of the action.

Here *continueth* to rot
The Body of *Francis Chartres*,
Who, with *Inflexible Conftancy*,
And inimitable Uniformity of Life,
Perfifted,
In fpite of Age and Infirmities,
In the Practice of every human Vice;
Excepting Prodigality and Hypocrify:
His infatiable Avarice exempted him from the firft,
His matchlefs Impudence from the fecond.
Nor was he more fingular
In the undeviating *Pravity* of his *Manners*,
Than fuccefsful
In *accumulating* Wealth;
For, without Trade or Profeffion,
Without Truft of Public Money,
And without Bribeworthy Service,
He acquired, or more properly created,
A Minifterial Eftate.
He was the only Perfon of his Time,
Who could cheat without the Mafk of Honefty.
He retain'd his primaeval Meannefs
When poffeffed of Ten Thoufand a Year;
And having daily deferved the Gibbet for what he *did*,
Was at laft condemned to it for what he *could* not *do*.
Oh, Indignant Reader!
Think not his Life ufelefs to Mankind!
PROVIDENCE permitted his execrable Defigns,
To give to after Ages
A confpicuous Proof and Example,
Of how fmall Eftimation is exorbitant Wealth
In the Sight of GOD,
By his beftowing it on the moft Unworthy of all Mortals.

Greyfriars Churchyard, Edinburgh

Here lies

Mals Andrew Gray

Of whom ne muckle good can I say

He was ne *Quaker* for he had ne spir^{it}

He was ne *Papist* for had ne merit

He was ne *Turk* for he drank muckle w^{ine}

He was ne *Jew* for he eat muckle sw^{ine}

Full forty years he preach^d & le'ed

For which *God* doomed him
                   when he de'ed

Died 11th October
1791

To the Memory of RICHARD HIND.
Here lies the Body of RICHARD HIND,
Who was neither ingenious, ſober, nor kind.

Cheshunt, Buckinghamshire

Here lies the body of Edward Hide.
We laid him here because he died.
   We had rather
   It had been his father.
   If it had been his sister,
   We should not have miss'd her.
   But since 'tis honest Ned
   No more shall be said.

A. 1817 D.

Storrington, Sussex

...e Harrifon, well known by the nam...

NANNA RAN DAN,

who was chafte but no prude;

& tho' free

yet no harlot.

By Principle vertuous,

by Education a Proteftant;

her freedom

made her liable to cenfure,

while her extenfive charities

made her efteemed.

Her tongue

fhe was unable to control,

but the reft of her members

fhe kept in fubjection.

After

a life of 80 years thus fpent,

fhe died.

1745.

Here lyeth
wrapt in Clay
The Body
of William Wray;
I have no more to fay.

St Michael's, Crooked Lane, London

On Susan Patison.

To free me from Domeſtic Strife,
Death call'd at my Houſe—but he ſpoke
With my Wife.
   Suſan, Wife of David Patiſon, lies here,
            Oct. 19, 1706.
Stop, Reader! and if not in a Hurry,
Shed a Tear.

Hadleigh, Suffolk

Walworth Churchyard, London A pun which would have been all too clear during the seventeenth century, when this inscription was engraved. 'To roger', say the contemporary dictionaries coyly, 'is to coit with a woman; derived from the name Roger which is generally given to a bull.'

HANNAH MARTIN

who died July 26 1716

Here lies the wife of
Roger Martin
She was a good wife
to Roger~ that's sartin

Beneath this Stone doth lie a Lafs,
   To Bucks and Bloods well known;
With any Man fhe'd drink a Glafs,
   And kifs for Half a Crown.

At fifteen Years fhe was a Whore,
   Was ten Years on the Town;
And would have ftood it many more,
   Had Death not knock'd her down.

An unlikely epitaph, taken from an eighteenth-century collection. Half a crown, for the information of the post-duodecimal generation, was 12½p. In the middle of that century it was a considerable sum, as is borne out by Thomas Arne's song, 'You're the Dearest Girl in Town' (. . . who would jump for half a crown. . . .).

On *Sir* JOHN GUISE

Here lies the Body of Sir *John Guiſe*,
Nobody laughs, and Nobody cries;
Where his Soul is, and how it fares,
Nobody knows, and Nobody cares.

Greyfriars Churchyard, Edinburgh

JESUS. MARIA.
GOD SAVE THE KING.

My aunceſtors have been interred here
  385 yeares
This by auntient evidence to mee appeares;
Which that all maye know & none doe
  offer wrong,
It is tenne ffotte broade & 4 yardes & a
  halfe longe.

Anno Domini 1661.
HENRY MOSOKE, Ætatis fuæ 14.
Ad Majorem Dei gloriam.
Richard Mofoke Sculpſit.

Aughton, Staffordshire

Here lies
DAME MARY PAGE,
Relict of Sir GREGORY PAGE, Bart.
Who departed this life March 4th, 1728,
In the 56th year of her age.
In 67 months she was tapped 66 times;
Had taken away 240 gallons of water,
Without ever repining at her case,
Or ever fearing the operation.

Bunhill Fields, London

I.O. 1591
In God is my whole truft.
John Orgen and Helen his wife.

As I was fo be ye: as I am you fhall be.
What I gaue, that I have,
What I fpent, that I had:
Thus I count all my coft,
That I left, that I loft.

St Olave's, Hart Street, London An inscription common from the sixteenth-century to the eighteenth century, and found in many parts of England, Scotland and Wales.

_In_
MEMORY OF

1 Two Grand-mothers with their two Grand-
   daughters,
2 Two Hufbands with their two Wives,
3 Two Fathers with their two Daughters,
4 Two Mothers with their two Sons,
5 Two Maidens with their two Mothers,
6 Two Sifters with their two Brothers:
Yet but fix Corpfes in all lye buried here,
All born legitimate, from Inceft clear.

EXPLANATION.

Two Widows that were Sifters-in-Law,
had each a Son, who married each other's
Mother, and by them had each a Daughter.

Suppofe one Widow's Name Mary, and her Son's Name John; and the other Widow's Name Sarah, and her Son's Name James. } This anfwers the 4th Line.

Then fuppofe John married Sarah, and had
a Daughter by her, and James married Mary,
and had a Daughter by her; thefe Marriages
anfwer the 1ft, 2d, 3d, 5th, and 6th Lines of
the Epitaph.

[_Arlington, near Paris._]

Greyfriars Church, Edinburgh

ear this place
lye the remains of

EDWARD BARKHAM Esq

Who in his liftime at his own expenſe
Erected the stately altarpiece in this Church
Furniſhed the Communion table
With a very rich crimſon velvet carpet
A cuſhion of the same & a beautiful Common Prayer book
Likewiſe with two large flagons
A chalice with a cover, together with a paten
All of silver plate
But above all (and what may very juſtly
preſerve his name to lateſt poſterity)
he gave and deviſed by will
to the Curate of Wainfleet St. Marys & his
succeſsors for ever
The sum of £35 per annum (over & above his former salary)
With this clauſe viz
'provided the said Curate & his succeſsors
do and shall read prayers and preach
once every Sunday in the year for ever.'
So extraordinary an inſtance of securing a
veneration for the moſt awful part of our religion
And so rare and uncommon a zeal
For promoting God's worſhip every Lord's day
(Divine Service being performed)
aforetime only every other Sunday.)

St George's Chapel, London This epitaph has been anthologized, quoted and re-anthologized in many corrupt and mutilated versions, including a shortened one, I regret to say, in *A Small Book of Grave Humour* (Pan Books). Since that book was published, I have been able to obtain the reliable text as copied in May 1877 by Thomas Ravenshaw. The subject of the inscription is not the fictitious 'Lady O'Looney' but Mrs Jane Molony.

SACRED TO THE MEMORY OF
MRS. JANE MOLONY
WHO LIES INTERRED
IN A VAULT UNDERNEATH THIS CHAPEL
DAUGHTER OF ANTONY SHEE
OF CASTLE BAR IN THE COUNTY OF MAYO ESQRE
WHO WAS MARRIED TO MISS BURKE
OF CURRY IN THE SAID COUNTY
AND COUSIN TO
THE RT HONBLE EDMOND BURKE
COMMONLY CALLED THE SUBLIME
WHOSE BUST IS HERE SURMOUNTED OR SUBJOINED
THE SAID JANE WAS COUSIN TO
THE LATE COUNTESS OF BUCKINGHAMSHIRE
AND WAS MARRIED TO
THREE SUCCESSIVE HUSBANDS
FIRST STUART ESQRE
COUSIN TO THE LATE MARQUIS OF BUTE;
SECONDLY TO WILLIAM COLLINS JACKSON
OF LANGLEY LODGE IN THE
COUNTY OF BUCKS FORMERLY MILITARY SECRETARY
TO THE HON: EAST INDIA COMPANY IN INDIA ESQRE
THIRDLY EDMOND MOLONY OF CLONONY CASTLE
KING'S COUNTY IRELAND ESQRE
BARRISTER AT LAW AND LATE,
OF WOODLANDS IN THE COUNTY OF DUBLIN

Cousin to the Earl of Roscommon,
who is brother in law of the
Present Earl of Shrewsbury
and also cousin of Lord Viscount Dillon
Of Costollo and Gallon in the Kingdom of Ireland
The first wife of the said
Edmond Molony was Jane Malone
Who is interred in the demesne of Barinstown
In the county of Westmeath with her
Brother in law Antony Malone Esqre,
and also with Her cousins
Lord Sunderlin And his predeceased brother
Edmond Malone commonly called
Shakspear Malone late of
Queen Anne Street East London
She was daughter of
Sergeant Richard Malone
an eminent lawyer and
A great statesman who possessed
great estates in the said king's county
And niece to the Rt. Honble Antony Malone
deceased Who was greatly Regretted
of whom it was said by one of
the most elegant writers Of the day
that he possessed one of the sweetest tongues
That ever uttered the dictates of reason

HE WAS A GREAT PATRIOT AND
REFUSED THE GREAT SEALS OF IRELAND
THE SITUATION BEING AT THE PLEASURE OF THE CROWN
WHILE CHANCELLOR OF THE EXCHEQUER
OF IRELAND FROM WHICH HE WAS REMOVED
WITHOUT CAUSE OR HIS OWN CONSENT
HE AVAILED HIMSELF OF THE
JUDICIAL PLACE ATTACHED TO IT
AND SAT ON THE BENCH ABOVE
THE CHIEF BARON AND DECIDED MANY CASES
WHICH GAVE GENERAL SATISFACTION
AND HIS DECREES WERE NEVER QUESTIONED
HE DIED 1776 AGED 76
THE SAID MRS MOLONY
OTHERWISE MALONE
DIED AT SAID WOODLANDS
IN FEBRUARY 1808 AGED 59
THE SAID MRS MOLONY
OTHERWISE SHEE DIED IN LONDON IN
JANUARY 1839
AGED 74
SHE WAS HOT PASSIONATE AND TENDER
AND A HIGHLY ACCOMPLISHED LADY
AND A SUPERB DRAWER IN WATER COLOURS
WHICH WAS MUCH ADMIRED IN THE
EXHIBITION ROOM IN SOMERSET HOUSE

SOME YEARS PAST
"THOUGH LOST FOR EVER, YET A FRIEND IS DEAR
THE HEART YET PAYS A TRIBUTARY TEAR."
THIS MONUMENT WAS ERECTED
BY HER DEEPLY AFFLICTED HUSBAND
THE SAID EDMOND MOLONY
IN MEMORY OF HER GREAT VIRTUES
AND TALENTS
BELOVED AND DEEPLY REGRETTED
BY ALL WHO KNEW HER
FOR OF SUCH IS THE KINGDOM OF HEAVEN.

THE evil that men do lives after them; the good
is often interred with their bones."

Here resteth the body of

THOMAS BATTYE

Late of Manchester,
Who died on a journey through Scotland
May 3d, 1793, aged 30.
This stone was placed here
By an acquaintance,
Who, after examining the *debits* and *credits*
Of his cash account,
Found a small balance in his favour.
His sickness was short,
And, being a stranger, he was not troubled in his last
moments with the sight of weeping friends,
But died at an inhospitable inn,
With the consent of all around him.
He left no mourner here,
Save a favourite mare; which,
(If the account of an ostler may be credited)
Neither ate nor drank during his indisposition.
READER!
Little will be said to perpetuate his memory;
The fact is—he died poor:
The whole he left behind, would not buy paper
Sufficient to paint half his virtues;
His chief mourner was sold by public roup,
To pay the expences of an overgrown landlord,
And an half-starved apothecary.
His bags at once contained
His *wardrobe, patterns, and library;*

Consisting of
Two neckcloths and a *clean shirt*;
With samples of
Fringes, laces, lines, and *tassels, whips, webs,*
and *whalebone.*
Also the following curious collection of books:
A volume of manuscript poetry,
(The offspring of his own muse)
Matrimonial magazines,
Ovid's Art of Love—The Whole Duty of Man, and
Plato on the Immortality of the Soul.
In a snug pocket,
Lay an Aberdeen note for five pounds,
And an unfinished love letter.
The latter evinced an eager desire of a
Speedy marriage;
For though his *family* face was an
Index of an hardened and unforgiving temper,
It was at last approved
By the object of his affection.
And if death had spared him, though
Nature had been unkind,
He might have lived to have improved an
Ill-favoured stock.
The affability of his manners,
And the susceptibility of his heart, gave
Appearances the lie:
His sympathetic feelings for distress
Were eminently displayed through life:
His attachment to the fair sex was notorious;
To whom he was so tenderly attentive,
That the story of a rude embrace would have caused

The "tear of sensibility" to
Trickle from his eye.*
He was ever happy in doing good,
And his liberality bountifully extended to
The unfortunate part of the sex,
Whom he always relieved to the utmost of
His power.
He was, justly speaking,
A friend to *all*;
And an enemy to none but *himself*.
BROTHER TRAVELLER,

STOP,

And reflect a moment
On the uncertainty of this life!
Five days are not yet passed, since he
Drank with glee,
The well-known bumper toast;
He little thought it was
His farewell tribute to every earthly pleasure!
But his last journey being o'er,
There is now
No riding double stages to make up lost time:
Nor boxing *Harry*
To make up his cash account.
Who knows but *Harry* may now be *boxing* him?
The final balance
Of the good and evil of his life
Is now stricken;
And here he rests in hope,
That it may be found to his *credit* on the
JUDGMENT DAY.
In the grand ledger of
EVERLASTING HAPPINESS!

* He had only one.

Here lies
the learned and facetious
Reverend WILLIAM GOODWIN
Fellow of Eton College and
Vicar of St Nicholas, who died
in June 1747. These written for
himself.

HERE lies a head that often ach'd;
Here lie two hands that always shak'd;
Here lies a brain of odd conceit;
Here lies a heart that often beat;
Here lie two eyes that daily wept,
And in the night but seldom slept;
Here lies a tongue that whining talk'd;
Here lie two feet that feebly walk'd;
Here lie the midriff, and the breast,
With loads of indigestion prest;
Here lies the liver full of bile,
That ne'er secreted proper chyle;
Here lie the bowels, human tripes,
Tortur'd with wind, and twisting gripes;
Here lies that livid dab, the spleen,
The source of life's sad tragic scene;

That left side weight that clogs the blood,
And stagnates nature's circling flood;
Here lie the nerves, so often twich'd
With painful cramps, and poignant stitch;
Here lies the back, oft rack'd with pains,
Corroding kidnies, loins, and reins;
Here lies the skin *per* scurvy fed,
With pimples, and eruptions red;
Here lies the man, from top to toe,
That fabric fam'd for pain and woe;
He caught a cold, but colder death
Compress'd his lungs and stopt his breath;
The organs could no longer go,
Because the bellows ceas'd to blow.

Thus I dissect this honest friend,
Who ne'er till death was at wit's end;
For want of spirits here he fell;
With higher spirits let him dwell,
In future state of peace and love,
Where just men's perfect spirits move.

Bristol